KNIGHTS AND CASTLES

Building a Castle

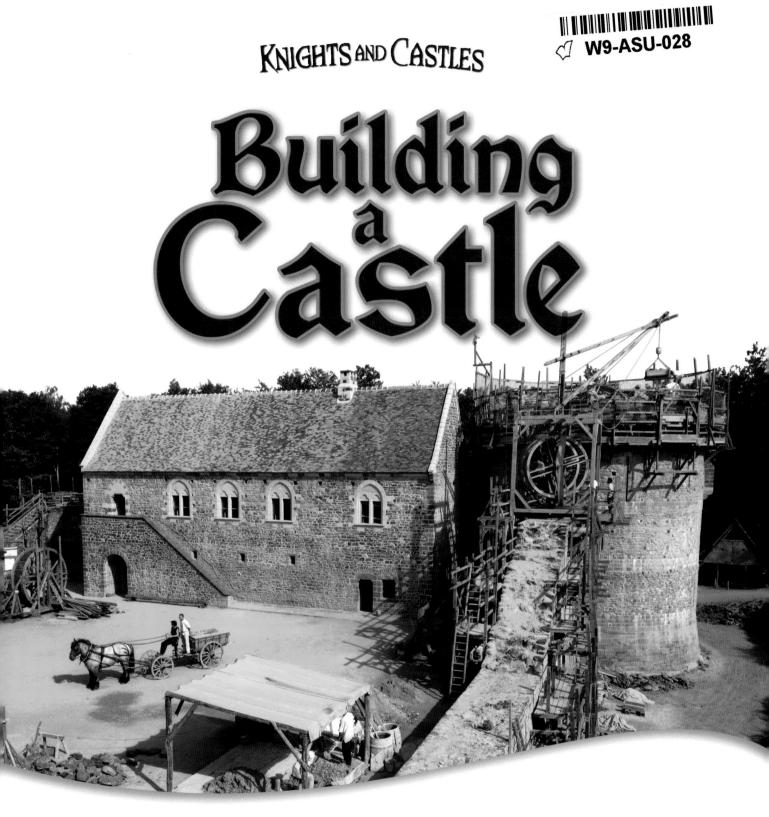

Paul Humphrey

ARCTURUS

This edition first published in 2012 by Arcturus Publishing

Distributed by Black Rabbit Books
P. O. Box 3263
Mankato
Minnesota MN 56002

Printed in the United States of America

Library of Congress Cataloging-in-Publication Data

Humphrey, Paul, 1952-
  Building a castle / by Paul Humphrey.
    pages cm -- (Knights and castles)
  Includes index.
  ISBN 978-1-84858-559-1 (hardcover, library bound)
  1. Castles--Europe--Design and construction--Juvenile literature. I. Title.
  NA7710.H86 2013
  728.8'1--dc23
                        2011051450

Series Concept: Discovery Books Ltd.
www.discoverybooks.net
Editor for Discovery Books: Laura Durman
Designer: Ian Winton

Picture credits: Château des Baux de Provence http://chateau-baux-provence.com p 18 (Culturespaces/ www.tophoto.fr.com/ Armedieval); Corbis pp 7 (Angelo Homak), 25b (Bettmann); Peter Dennis pp 8t, 10t, 15; Getty Images cover and p 17 (Gamma-Rapho), pp 9 (Hulton Archive), 12 (Gamma-Rapho), 14 (Gamma-Rapho), 22 (Gamma-Rapho), 23 (Gamma-Rapho); Guédelon Chantier Médiéval title page and pp 21 (Michel Adnot), 26b (Christian Duchemin); Photoshot p 10b (Steve Vidler); Shutterstock Images pp 4 (topal), 5 (Rostislav Glinsky), 6 (Bill McKelvie), 8b (Stanislaw Tokarski), 11 (St. Nick), 13 (San Strickler), 19t (steve estvanik), 19b(Nick Hawkes), 20 (vadim kozlovsky), 24 (Euro Colour Creative), 25t (Platslee), 26t (Péter Gudella), 27 (vitek12), 28 (m.bonotto); Wikimedia pp 16, 29t.

Every attempt has been made to clear copyright. Should there be any inadvertent omission, please apply to the publisher for rectification.

SL002130US
Supplier 02, Date 1213, Print run 3193

Contents

What is a castle?

A castle is a **fortified** home of a lord or king. Most of the castles that survive today were made of stone, with thick walls surrounding a strong "keep" in the middle. These castles were built in Europe between the 11th and 15th centuries (600 to 1,000 years ago) during a time called the **Middle Ages**.

Ancient times

The very first fortified homes and towns were built in ancient times. Around 1800 BC (nearly 4,000 years ago) the Egyptians built a string of forts with stone walls in a part of their **empire** called Nubia. Nebuchadnezzar II built the fortified city of Babylon around 600 BC with walls that were more than 20 feet (6 m) thick!

Lords often allowed wealthy knights to build houses on their land. In return the knights would protect the lord and his castle during a siege.

Europe one thousand years ago was very different from the place we know now. There were no real roads and few big cities, just small towns and villages. The countryside was made up mostly of forests, marshes, and farmland. It was also a lawless place, and there were often battles between rival lords and kings. They needed somewhere to protect themselves and the people who worked for them.

BIGGEST CASTLE

The largest castle in the world is in Prague, in the Czech Republic. Hradcany Castle covers an more than 30 acres (7 ha). It contains an entire cathedral.

Cathedral

Perhaps the best time to appreciate Hradcany Castle is at night, when it is beautifully lit above the city. St. Vitus Cathedral can be seen towering above the castle walls.

Hill forts

The Celts of northern Europe lived more than 2,000 years ago. They built hill forts to protect themselves against neighboring tribes. There are many similarities between these early forts and **medieval** castles.

Early hill forts were made from earth. The Celts used spades and picks to dig deep, circular ditches. The earth they dug out was piled up into high **ramparts**. There were usually only one or two entrances into a hill fort. Attackers had to charge up and down the ramparts to get into the fort, braving the defenders' spears, stones, and arrows. Later forts were made from wood or stone.

The ruins of the Dun Carloway Broch hill fort can still be seen on the Isle of Lewis, Scotland. It was probably the home of a tribal leader.

Maiden Castle (not really a castle) in southern England was one of the biggest hill forts ever made. It was built around 300 BC. Its ramparts were 20 feet (6 m) high and it was more than 2 miles (3 km) in circumference. Maiden Castle was more than just a fort, though. It was a whole town, with houses, granaries, stores, and other buildings. Its defenses were no match for the Roman armies, however. The hill fort was overrun in AD 43, and its inhabitants were either killed or taken captive.

This aerial photograph shows the full extent of the Maiden Castle hill fort.

BEACH WEAPONS
Archaeologist Sir Mortimer Wheeler **excavated** Maiden Castle the in the 1930s and found 22,000 pebbles from a beach 2 miles (5 km) away. These were fired from **slings** used as by the Celts.

Motte and bailey castles

The first true castles in western Europe were built 1,100-1,200 years ago. They were called motte and bailey castles.

The 9th and 10th centuries AD were a time of great lawlessness. Lords offered to protect local villagers in exchange for their land. The lords built up an army of soldiers and housed them in fortified buildings, surrounded by a wooden **palisade**. This enclosed an area called the bailey, which was itself often encircled by a ditch.

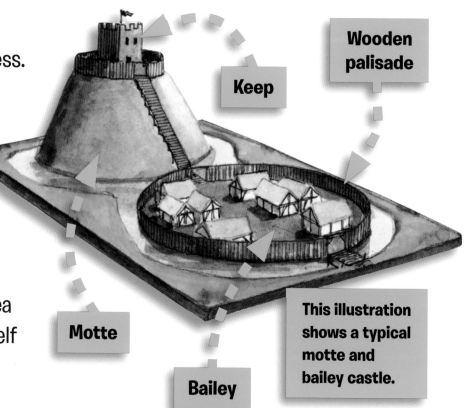

Keep

Wooden palisade

Motte

Bailey

This illustration shows a typical motte and bailey castle.

If invaders managed to get across the ditch and over the palisade, the defending villagers and soldiers would rush to the keep. This was a strong wooden building, usually built on a natural or man-made hill, called a motte.

An attacking army approaches a castle. It was easier for castle defenders to see enemies from a long distance away if the keep was built on top of a hill.

Do-it-yourself Castles

The Normans came from northern France. They invaded and conquered Saxon Britain in 1066. They built lots of motte and bailey castles. The Normans forced the conquered Saxon slaves to build the castles. Usually they used wood from local forests. However, the castles were needed in such a hurry that timber was sometimes cut in Normandy. It was sent with the pegs and nails across the English Channel to be assembled in England, a bit like the do-it-yourself furniture kits you can buy today!

This section of the **Bayeux Tapestry** shows Saxon slaves building a castle.

CASTLES EVERYWHERE

Within 100 years of the Norman conquest, around 600 motte and bailey castles had been built across England and Wales.

Stone castles

The trouble with wooden castle keeps, surrounded by wooden palisades, was that they could be burned down. The wood also got damp and rotted. Stronger, stone castles were needed.

The first stone castles were built on the sites of the old motte and bailey ones. A square stone keep replaced the wooden one. Polygonal (or many-sided) keeps could have six or even eight sides, while round keeps were circular. Some castles had no keep at all, just a high stone wall with stone and wooden buildings inside.

Stone castles were much stronger than wooden ones. They were built from the end of the 11th century.

CASTLE COLLECTORS
Medieval lords and kings often owned more than one castle. England's King John owned more than 100.

This statue of King John was part of a display at King John's Castle in Limerick, Ireland, one of the many castles that he owned.

Over time, castles became more and more elaborate. Towers were built at intervals along the walls. Gatehouses, or barbicans, protected the entrances. **Concentric** castles had two or more walls, with the inner ones higher than those on the outside. This meant archers could fire down on their enemies.

Windsor castle has many elaborate gateways such as this one. Having two towers meant that soldiers could shower attackers with arrows from either side of the gate.

Inside the castle walls were other buildings necessary for the running of the castle. There might be a blacksmith's **forge**, stables, a chapel, and workshops for the castle craftsmen. These were usually made of a framework of wooden beams. Flexible panels of hazel twigs, called wattle, filled in the gaps between the beams. The wattles were daubed with a mixture of wet soil, clay, sand, animal dung, and straw. The buildings were roofed with thatch.

Planning a castle

The first thing a lord had to do if he was planning on building a castle was to count up his money. Castles were very expensive to construct and the final cost would have been the medieval equivalent of millions of dollars in today's money. They also took a long time to build (up to 20 years or more).

A master mason surveys his chosen site as the castle walls begin to take shape.

The most important person in the construction team was the master **mason**, also known as the master of works. He acted as the chief **architect** and **surveyor**. The master mason also managed all the other people involved in the project, and made sure it did not go over budget.

Quite a team

"In case you should wonder where so much money could go in a week, we would have you know that we have needed 400 masons... 2,000 less skilled workmen, 100 carts, 60 wagons, and 30 boats bringing stone and sea coal; 200 quarrymen; 30 smiths; and carpenters for putting in the joists and floorboards and other necessary jobs."

From Master James of St. George (King Edward I's master mason) concerning the building of Beaumaris Castle in Wales.

WHERE TO BUILD

The master mason would advise the lord on the best place to build the castle.
He had a number of things to think about, because castles had to be:

- In a good defensive position on a hill, a bend in a river, or on the coast
- Near a good supply of food and fuel
- Near a quarry for digging out the stone and/or to a river or the sea for transporting it
- Within a day's walk of the lord's lands
- Built on a place with solid foundations so the castle didn't fall down
- Near a source of clean drinking water
- Near a good source of wood

Dunnottar Castle in Scotland was built in an excellent defensive position. During the 17th century, soldiers held out for eight months while the castle was under siege. By doing this, they saved the Scottish crown jewels from destruction.

Quarrying and cutting the stone

Digging out stone was hard and dangerous work. Quarrymen worked long hours by candlelight using only hand tools such as picks and saws. Often child labor was used as it was cheap.

Stone for making a castle was usually taken from quarries nearby. Limestone or sandstone was preferred. The blocks of stone were lifted by hand-operated cranes and loaded onto horse-drawn wagons. If they had to be carried some distance, they would be taken to barges on a nearby river or to a seaport.

Slabs of stone are unloaded from a horse-drawn wagon at the castle building site. These slabs will be cut and shaped by stonemasons.

Stonemasons worked under the guidance of the master mason. The rough mason simply cut the stone into blocks. Skilled masons shaped the blocks into ashlar–the regular, flat-faced shapes used for most castle building. Others carved intricate patterns on doors, windows, and other decorations.

The stonemason's tools

Stonemasons used a variety of different chisels. The pitcher was used for roughing out a shape from a stone slab. The point or punch chisel and the claw chisel were used to get rid of unnecessary bits of stone and reduce the block to the required size. The straight chisel was used to get the final surface and also to add the mason's marks to the block. A lump hammer of metal, or a wooden mallet, was used to strike the chisels. Stonemasons also used **dividers**, a **set square**, and a straight edge, just like modern builders.

The master mason supervises work on a stone block. He holds dividers, while the stonemason uses a claw chisel and lump hammer.

Building the walls

There were no diesel or electric engines, bulldozers, or mechanical cranes in medieval times. All the heavy lifting work had to be done by hand. But there were simple machines to help builders, even hundreds of years ago.

Cranes were powered by **treadmills**. These were rather like a hamster wheel but with men inside doing the walking. Ladders were used to reach the lower parts of the walls, but to get to the highest parts, scaffolding had to be erected. This was made of wooden poles, and was not nearly as safe as the metal scaffolding used today. Accidents were common. Putlog holes up the sides of the walls helped to support one end of the scaffolding poles.

A treadmill is used to lift heavy stone to the top of the castle wall. On the ground, stonemasons work to shape rough blocks into ashlar.

The walls were built rather like a sandwich. Neatly trimmed blocks of ashlar formed the outer sides. This was infilled with stones and rubble. A **plumb bob** and plumb line were used to ensure the walls were vertical.

LIME MORTAR

Lime mortar held everything together. This was a mix of lime, sand, and water. The lime was **extracted** from limestone or chalk by heating it to 1,600°F (900°C) in a furnace called a lime kiln. It took a week to load, fire, and remove the lime.

Workers build a castle wall and staircase. A stonemason chisels away the stones' sharp corners.

Castle defenses

There was more to castle building than just making walls Castles had lots of defensive features that made it more difficult for attackers to get in.

Castle walls were usually thicker at the base to make them less likely to collapse when hit by battering rams. They were also sloped at the bottom so that stones and other missiles hurled from above would bounce off them and hit attacking soldiers.

Castle walls had to be thick to have any chance of withstanding the missiles launched from large siege weapons such as this one.

At the top of every wall were the battlements or crenellations. The merlon (the solid part) gave archers something to hide behind while they reloaded. Then they could fire through the gap, or crenel. The inner walkways along the side of the battlements were built narrow enough for just a few men. Any attackers making their way over the battlements were thus vulnerable to attack from defenders inside the walls.

Mamure Castle in Turkey features narrow walkways and crenellations along the castle walls. The crenellations would have protected archers as they reloaded their weapons.

Wooden hoardings were often built at the tops of walls and towers. These overhung the walls and allowed archers to get a better view of the attackers below. Unfortunately, these could be set on fire, so they were later replaced with stone machicolations.

This photograph shows the view up to machicolations at Lewes Castle in Sussex, England.

MURDER!

Castle builders left openings in the floor above the gate passage. These "murder holes" could be used to hurl stones, fire-heated sand, or burning pieces of wood down on attacking soldiers.

Ironwork

Iron had many uses in the castles of the Middle Ages. It was used to make hinges, locks, keys, and reinforcing bars for doors. Iron nails held floorboards and wooden hoardings in place. It was also often used for the portcullis, a latticed grille that could be raised or lowered to seal off the gateway to a castle.

Nails, nails

In 1327 the stock of nails in York castle numbered 43,000.

The strong iron bars nailed to this wooden door would have made it more difficult for battering rams to smash through it.

Iron ore was dug from **open-cast** pits and crushed using the power from **watermills**. Watermills were also used to blow air into iron **smelters**, where the pure iron was extracted from the rocky ore. Water powered the machines that hammered the molten iron into rough shapes, too.

Medieval smiths mostly worked with **wrought iron**. The iron was heated to around 1,300°F (700°C). At this temperature it could be beaten into shape–flat strips for hinges and reinforcements and long lengths of wire, which could then be cut and hammered into nails.

Blacksmiths were a very important part of castle life as they made and repaired tools, weapons, and armor, among other things.

EXPENSIVE IRON

Iron was very costly to make, so it was used sparingly. In the furnace of an iron smelter a whole oak tree would have to be burned to make just 55 pounds (25 kg) of iron.

Iron was also used to make tools for the other craftsmen employed in the construction of a castle, such as stonemasons and carpenters.

Woodwork

Wood was used to make the original motte and bailey castles and palisades as well as the buildings within. But even when stone replaced wood as the main material for castle building, the carpenter's skills were still in great demand.

Wood was used to make roofs and hoardings, doors and floors, and the framework for the buildings inside the castle walls. It was taken from local forests by sawyers (people who saw wood) and cut into lengths to be transported by cart to the castle site. There it was shaped into the planks, beams, and pegs needed for castle construction.

Once a building site was chosen, sawyers were employed to clear any trees or bushes away. They would also collect and saw timber for use in building the castle.

Sawyers used different kinds of saws for different types of work. A two-man bow saw might be used to cut down the length of a tree trunk to make planks and beams. Smaller saws would be used for more intricate work. Round wooden pegs were made on a simple **lathe** powered by a foot **treadle**. The pegs were used to fix beams together.

Once the castle was built, carpenters were kept busy making tool handles, furniture, bowls, wheels, and frames for shields as well as repairing floorboards and doors.

Shingles (tiles) for roofs were made by splitting oak logs into thin sheets. These were fixed on to the wooden frame with iron nails.

Costly carpenters

Everything had to fit together exactly on a medieval building, and carpenters were among the most skilled and well-paid workers on a castle construction site. Once a lord had found a good carpenter, he would try to keep him on his staff.

Digging the moat

Castles built on high, rocky cliffs or by the sea had a natural defense from enemies. Other castles were more vulnerable to attack from battering rams and **undermining**. The solution to such threats was a moat.

A moat was a deep ditch surrounding a castle. Moats were sometimes filled with sharp stakes to deter attacking forces and their horses. Better still, though, they could be filled with water.

Muiderslot Castle in Holland was built on flat land with no natural defenses. To help protect it, the castle is surrounded by a large moat.

MOAT MYTHS

There are many legends and myths surrounding castle moats. People believed there were dragons or other fierce creatures living in them. Perhaps castle dwellers said this to further deter would-be attackers. Most moats, however, were filled only with disgustingly smelly water, which was usually enough.

The moat was dug by hand, usually by the lord's servants and local peasants. It was then connected to a local water source, such as a lake, stream, or river, and filled with water. A wooden **sluice gate** would be added to stop the moat overflowing.

Few soldiers could swim in the Middle Ages, and crossing the moat in a rowboat with archers raining arrows down was dangerous work. To make matters worse, the castle's toilets usually emptied into the moat, and if the defenders knew they were about to be attacked they would fill the moat with rotting animals and other nasties to deter unwanted bathers.

All 28 toilets in Bodiam Castle emptied into its large moat, so enemies would not have been keen to take a swim in it.

Tall siege towers were wheeled up to castle walls, allowing the enemy soldiers inside to climb over the battlements. Placing a moat around the castle made this type of attack more difficult. Besiegers had to fill the moat with rocks before they could reach the walls.

Doors and windows

Castles were designed for defense. For this reason, they were built with as few openings as necessary.

The main castle entrance across the moat might be protected by a drawbridge. This was made of stout wood, with iron reinforcement and was hinged, so it could be quickly drawn up when enemies approached. Behind the drawbridge was the portcullis (see page 20).

The main gates of the castle were bolted shut at night, even during peacetime. A smaller gate within the main gate-called the wicket gate-could be opened to let visitors in.

The wicket gates within this main gate would have been used to allow visitors into the castle at night.

Over the doors, stone masons often made decorative arches from carefully carved stone. These were supported by a wooden frame during construction, which was then removed when the arch was complete.

The blocks of stone that make up this arched window have been cut to size and are being carefully positioned by masons.

Windows, too, were made more for defense than to let in light, especially those lower down the castle walls. Called arrow loops, these slit windows were no more than one or two inches wide. But they broadened out on the inside. This made it difficult for attacking archers to fire in, but easy for defenders to take aim and shoot arrows out. Some arrow loops also had slits across them. This gave defending archers a wider range of fire.

Arrow loop

Portcullis

This gate at Arundel Castle features an iron portcullis that would be lowered to keep enemies out. In the tower above are arrow loops from which archers could fire on enemies.

Glass was extremely expensive during the Middle Ages, and was reserved for the castle chapel, and, sometimes, for the lord's living quarters. Wooden shutters helped keep out drafts.

Castle comforts

Castles were built for strength and protection. But rich lords also wanted to impress visitors with their wealth. As the Middle Ages progressed, castles gradually became more and more comfortable places to live in.

The walls inside Malpaga Castle in Italy are almost all covered in beautiful paintings called frescoes. King Christian I of Denmark visited the castle in 1474 and many of the frescoes celebrate this event.

Castle walls might contain carvings made by talented sculptors. In some castles, highly skilled plasterers smoothed over the rough stones. Painters then decorated them with bright colors and designs. Wooden beams were often highlighted in gold paint.

The chapel was the most beautiful place in the castle. It might have stained glass windows, highly decorated arches and walls, and beautiful floor tiles in medieval patterns.

Colorful **tapestries** were hung from castle walls, and also used to divide bedrooms. **Crusaders** returning from the Middle East brought back colorful carpets, which were often considered too precious to be used on the floor. Instead they adorned walls and tables. Cheaper wool rugs, rush matting, or straw were the usual floor coverings.

This tapestry is part of a collection displayed at Wawel Castle in Poland. Tapestries decorated the walls of medieval castles, especially in the great hall and the lord's bedroom.

THE ARRAS

The best tapestries came from Arras, in northern France. They were known as Arras Cloth, or just the Arras. Large tapestries of the finest cloth could take five weavers up to eight months to make. They were definitely for the wealthy only.

Skilled carpenters and cabinetmakers completed the furnishing of the castle. They made elaborately carved wooden chests for storing clothes and valuables, tables and chairs, as well as beds for the lord and his lady.

Two skilled carpenters make carved ornaments out of wood.

Glossary

aerial photograph a photograph taken from an aircraft

archaeologist someone who studies buildings, bones, and other remains of the past

architect someone who designs buildings

Bayeux Tapestry an embroidered cloth, 230 feet (70 m) long, which illustrates the Norman conquest of England

concentric describes a set of shapes, one inside the other

Crusader a knight who joined the Crusades, a series of wars fought in the Middle East between Christians and Muslims in the 11th to 13th centuries

dividers a tool with two movable points used for scribing circles

empire the total area of a country or countries ruled by one country

excavate to remove or uncover something by digging

extract to remove or take out

forge a place where blacksmiths make ironware

fortified reinforced, strengthened

lathe a turning machine on which wood or metal can be shaped

mason a craftsman who works in stone

medieval describes the period of the Middle Ages in Europe from the 5th to the 15th centuries

Middle Ages the medieval period of history, between the 5th century and the 15th century

open-cast describes a form of mining where the top layer of soil and rock is removed to get at the minerals below

palisade a defensive wall

plumb bob a weight attached to a plumb line, used to make sure that buildings are vertical

rampart a defensive wall

set square a tool in which two strips of wood or metal are set at a right angle to make sure that an angle is square

siege an attack by enemy forces in which a castle is cut off from supplies

sling a weapon using a looped strap that is swung quickly, sending stones flying off

sluice gate a gate across a stream that can be opened or shut to let water in or out

smelter a furnace for extracting iron from iron ore

surveyor someone who inspects the plot of land and draws plans for a building

tapestry a picture made of embroidered threads

treadle a pedal which, when moved up and down, turns a wheel

treadmill a circular framework in which people or animals walked to turn machines

undermining a tactic used by attacking forces in which a tunnel was dug under the castle wall and set alight, causing the wall to collapse

watermill a building in which the energy of moving water is used to turn a wheel and power machines

wrought iron a form of molten iron which can be hammered into different shapes

Further reading

Castle (DK Eyewitness) by Christopher Gravett (DK Children, 2008)

Castles by Stephanie Turnbull (Usborne, 2007)

Castles (Medieval Warfare) by Deborah Murrell (World Almanac Library, 2008)

Did Castles Have Bathrooms? by Ann Kerns (Lerner, 2010)

Everything Castles by Crispin Boyer (National Geographic Kids, 2011)

The World's Most Amazing Castles by Ann Weil (Raintree, 2011)

What Were Castles For? by Phil Roxbee Cox (Usborne, 2002)

Websites

http://www.castles.me.uk/medieval-castles.htm
Explore medieval life in a castle on this informative website, which also has details of how castles were built and how much they cost.

http://castles-of-britain.com/buildingacastle.htm
Find out how much it cost to build some of the biggest medieval castles.

http://www.castles.org/Kids_Section/Castle_Story
Find out what goes on inside a castle on this interesting website.

http://www.pictures-of-castles.co.uk
Find hundreds of pictures of different castles around Britain.

http://www.guedelon.fr/en/
Visit this site to see a medieval castle being built in modern France.

Index